CENGAGE Learning

Drama for Students, Volume 23

Project Editors: Sara Constantakis and Ira Mark Milne Editorial: Anne Marie Hacht

Rights Acquisition and Management: Sue Rudolph, Jessica Schultz, Timothy Sisler Manufacturing: Drew Kalasky

Imaging: Leitha Etheridge-Sims, Lezlie Light, Mike Logusz Product Design: Pamela A. E. Galbreath Vendor Administration: Civie Green

Product Manager: Meggin Condino

For more information, contact
Gale, an imprint of Cengage Learning
27500 Drake Rd.
Farmington Hills, MI 48331-3535
Or you can visit our Internet site at

ISBN 0-7876-6945-8

ISSN 1094-3552

Printed in the United States of America
10 9 8 7 6 5 4 3 2 1

Twelve Angry Men

Reginald Rose 1954

Introduction

Twelve Angry Men, by the American playwright Reginald Rose, was originally written for television, and it was broadcast live on CBS's show *Studio One* in 1954. The fifty-minute television script can be found in Rose's *Six Television Plays*, published in 1956 (out of print in 2005). Rose expanded the play for the stage, and a new version was published in 1955 (Dramatic Publishing Company; in print). Two years later, in 1957, Rose wrote the screenplay for a film version, which he coproduced with the actor Henry Fonda. The play has subsequently been updated and revived; for example, in a production at the American Airlines Theater in New York City in 2004.

The play was inspired by Rose's own experience of jury duty on a manslaughter case in New York City. At first, he had been reluctant to serve on a jury, but, he wrote, "the moment I walked into the courtroom ... and found myself facing a strange man whose fate was suddenly more or less in my hands, my entire attitude changed." Rose was greatly impressed by the gravity of the situation, the somber activity of the court, and the "absolute finality" of the decision that he and his fellow jurors would have to make. He also thought that since no one other than the jurors had any idea of what went on in a jury room, "a play taking place entirely within a jury room might be an exciting and possibly moving experience for an audience" ("Author's Commentary" on *Twelve Angry Men* in *Six Television Plays*). The result is a taut, engrossing drama in which eleven jurors believe the defendant in a capital murder trial is guilty, while one juror stands up courageously for what he believes is justice and tries to persuade the others to his way of thinking.

Author Biography

Reginald Rose was born on December 10, 1920, in New York City, the son of William (a lawyer) and Alice (Obendorfer) Rose. Rose attended City College (now of the City University of New York) from 1937 to 1938 but did not graduate. During World War II and shortly after, he served in the U.S. Army, from 1942 to 1946, ending his army career as a first lieutenant. In 1943, Rose married Barbara Langbart, and they had four children.

After the war and continuing into the early 1950s, Rose worked as a clerk, publicity writer for Warner Brothers Pictures, and advertising copywriter. He also wrote short stories and novels, but he never had any luck selling his work until he turned to writing plays for television. CBS bought the first script he wrote, called *The Bus to Nowhere*, and it aired live in 1951. He then became a regular writer for CBS's *Studio One*, a weekly show that produced live drama. His plays for *Studio One* included *Dino, The Death and Life of Larry Benson, The Remarkable Incident at Carson Corners*, and *Thunder on Sycamore Street*, all of which aired in 1954. In the same year, Rose wrote *Twelve Angry Men*, the work for which he is best known. The play, which was inspired by his experience of jury service, was broadcast on September 20, 1954. It won an Emmy Award for best-written drama and a Writer's Guild of America Award. The teleplay was published in Rose's *Six Television Plays* in 1956.

Twelve Angry Men was published in an expanded form as a stage play in 1955 and made into a successful film in 1957, starring Henry Fonda and coproduced by Fonda and Rose. The film garnered Academy Award nominations for Best Picture, Best Director, and Best Writing, Screenplay Based on Material from Another Medium, and an Edgar Allan Poe Award for Best Motion Picture Screenplay from Mystery Writers of America.

Rose continued to write television scripts during the 1960s and beyond. One of his best-known shows was the series *The Defenders* (1961–1965), about a father-and-son team of defense lawyers. Other shows included *A Quiet Game of Cards* (1959), the *Studs Lonigan* miniseries (1979), *Escape from Sobibor* (1987), and made-for-television movies of *Twelve Angry Men* and *The Defenders: Taking the First* in the 1990s.

Rose wrote five plays for the stage, including *Black Monday* in 1962 and *This Agony, This Triumph* in 1972, as well as several rewrites of *Twelve Angry Men* (1960, 1964, and 1996). He also wrote eleven screenplays besides *Twelve Angry Men*, including *Somebody Killed Her Husband* (1978), *The Wild Geese* (1978; based on a novel by Daniel Carney), and *Whose Life Is It Anyway?* (1981), starring Richard Dreyfuss.

Rose's first marriage ended in divorce. He married his second wife, Ellen McLaughlin, in 1963; they had two children. He died on April 19, 2002, in Norwalk, Connecticut.

Plot Summary

Act 1

Twelve Angry Men takes place in a jury room in the late afternoon on a hot summer's day in New York City. After the curtain rises, the judge's voice is heard offstage, giving instructions to the jury. He says that the defendant is being tried for first-degree murder, which carries a mandatory death penalty. The judge adds that if the jury has reasonable doubt about the guilt of the accused, they must acquit him. The verdict must be unanimous.

The jurors, all men, file into the jury room and sit in straight-backed chairs around a long conference table. The weather is hot, and there is no air-conditioning; some of the men are irritable. From the initial chitchat, it is clear that most members of the jury regard the man as guilty. Jurors Seven and Ten ridicule the defendant's story. Apparently, a young man has stabbed his father to death with a knife. He admits that he bought a knife that night but claims that he lost it.

The jury takes a vote. Eleven jurors vote guilty, and one juror, Juror Eight, votes not guilty. Jurors Three, Seven, and Twelve criticize him, but Juror Eight says that he does not know whether the man is guilty or not but that it is not easy for him to send a boy to his death without discussing it first. After some argument, they agree to discuss the facts of the case. Juror Three reviews what they know. An old man who lives underneath the room where the murder took place heard loud noises just after midnight. He heard the son yell at the father that he was going to kill him. Then he heard a body falling and moments later, saw the boy running out of the house. Juror Four says the boy's story is flimsy. He said that he was at the movies at the time of the murder, but no one remembers seeing him there. Also, a woman living opposite looked out of her window and saw the murder through the windows of a passing elevated train. During the trial, it was verified that this was possible. Further facts emerge: the father regularly beat his son, and the son had been arrested for car theft, mugging, and knife fighting. He had been sent to reform school for knifing someone.

Juror Eight insists that, during the trial, too many questions were left unasked. He asks for the murder weapon to be brought in and says that it is possible that someone else stabbed the boy's father with a similar knife. Several jurors insist the knife is a very unusual one, but then Juror Eight produces from his pocket a switchblade that is exactly the same. He says that it is possible the boy is telling the truth. The other jurors scoff at this, but Juror Eight calls for another vote, a secret one this time. He says that he will abstain. When the votes are counted, there are ten guilty votes and one not guilty.

Media Adaptations

- In 1957, *Twelve Angry Men* was made into a film starring Henry Fonda and Lee J. Cobb and directed by Sydney Lumet, with a screenplay by Rose (produced by Orion-Nova Productions/United Artists). It is available on DVD through MGM/UA Video.

- In 1997, the cable channel Showtime released the made-for-television movie of *Twelve Angry Men*, directed by William Friedkin and starring Jack Lemmon as Juror Eight, with George C. Scott, Hume Cronyn, James Gandolfini, and Tony Danza. Rose produced an updated screenplay for this production. The videotape, put out by MGM/UA

Act 2

Juror Three is angry with Juror Five because he thinks that Juror Five is the one who changed his vote. It transpires that the not-guilty vote was cast by Juror Nine. This juror says that he wants to hear more discussion of the case, even though there is still a strong feeling among the other jurors that the defendant is guilty. Jurors Three and Twelve start to play a game of tic-tac-toe to pass the time, but Juror Eight angrily snatches the piece of paper away, saying that jury deliberations are not a game. Pressured by Juror Eight, the jury agrees that it would take about ten seconds for the train to pass by the apartment. Juror Eight also establishes that the train is noisy, so the old man could not have heard the boy yell that he was going to kill his father, as the old man testified. Juror Nine suggests that the old man may have convinced himself that he heard the words because he has never had any recognition from anyone and has a strong need for attention. Juror Three responds to this with hostility, but Juror Eight argues additionally that even if the boy had said he was going to kill his father, that does not mean he intended to do so, since people often use that or similar phrases without meaning them. Convinced by these arguments, Juror Five changes his vote to not guilty, making the vote nine to three.

Juror Eight then questions the old man's

testimony that he took only fifteen seconds to get downstairs, open the front door, and see the boy fleeing. He says that bearing in mind that the man cannot walk well, it probably took longer. Using a diagram of the apartment, Juror Eight acts out the old man's steps and is timed at thirty-nine seconds. He says that the old man must have heard, rather than seen, someone racing down the stairs and assumed it was the boy. An argument erupts between Jurors Three and Eight, as Juror Three insists the boy is guilty and must be executed. Juror Eight accuses him of being a sadist. Juror Three lunges at him, screaming that he will kill him. Juror Eight replies softly, suggesting that perhaps Juror Three does not really mean what he is saying.

Act 3

The jurors take another vote, this time an open one, which is evenly split, six to six. Jurors Two, Six, and Eleven have switched their votes, to the annoyance of Jurors Three and Ten. The possibility of being a hung jury is brought up, but Juror Eight refuses to accept the possibility. They take a vote on that, too. Six jurors vote in favor of declaring themselves a hung jury; six vote against. Juror Four changes his vote, so it is seven to five against declaring a hung jury. Juror Four then argues persuasively for a guilty verdict, based on the evidence. He raises the possibility that although the old man may have taken longer to get to the door than he testified, the murderer might also have taken longer to escape. Reenacting the actions of the murderer, the jurors time it at twenty-nine and a half seconds. This suggests that the old man's testimony that he saw the boy fleeing may be correct after all. As a result, three jurors change their votes back, leaving the tally at nine to three in favor of guilt.

Juror Two raises a question about the fact that the fatal wound was caused by a downward thrust of the knife. How could that be, since the son is six inches shorter than his father, which would make such an action very awkward? Juror Three demonstrates on Juror Eight how it could be done, crouching down to approximate the boy's height and then raising the knife and making a downward stabbing motion. But Juror Five, who has witnessed knife fights, says that anyone using a switchblade would use it underhand, stabbing upward, thus making it unlikely that the boy, who was an experienced knife fighter, could have caused the fatal wound. Another vote is taken, and it is nine to three in favor of acquittal. Juror Ten goes off on a prejudiced rant about how all people from the slums are liars and violent and have no respect for human life. Disgusted with his views, most of the other jurors get up and walk to the window, where they turn their backs on Juror Ten.

Juror Four still insists that the boy is guilty. He says the most important testimony is that of the woman who says she saw the murder. She was in bed, unable to sleep, when she looked out the window and saw the boy stab his father. Juror Eight reminds them that the woman wears glasses, but she would not wear them in bed and would not have had time to put them on to see what she claims to have seen. He contends that she could have seen only a blur. At this, Jurors Four and Ten change their votes to not guilty, leaving the tally at eleven to one. Only Juror Three insists on a guilty verdict, but when he sees that he stands alone and cannot change anyone else's opinion, he begrudgingly votes not guilty. The jury has reached a unanimous decision, and the defendant is acquitted.

Characters

Foreman

The foreman is described in the author's notes to the play as "a small, petty man who is impressed with the authority he has." The foreman tries to run the meeting in an orderly fashion, but in the film he is too sensitive and sulks when his attempt to stick to the way they had agreed to proceed is questioned. His contribution to the deliberations comes when they are discussing how long the killer would have taken to get downstairs. The foreman points out that since the killer wiped his fingerprints off the knife, he would also have done so off the doorknob, which would have taken some time. He votes guilty several times, but in act 3 he switches his vote, along with two others, to make the total nine to three for acquittal.

Juror Two

Juror Two is a quiet, meek figure who finds it difficult to maintain an independent opinion. In the 1957 film, he is a bank clerk. Juror Two does, however, make one useful contribution to the jury deliberations. He mentions that it seems awkward that the defendant, who was six inches shorter than his father, would stab him with a downward motion, as the fatal wound indicates. Although this is not a conclusive point, it does jog Juror Five's memory of how a switchblade is used and so helps to induce doubt in the minds of a number of jurors. Juror Two changes his vote to not guilty at the beginning of act 3, along with Jurors Eleven and Six.

Juror Three

Juror Three is a forceful, intolerant man who is also a bully. In the 1957 film, he runs a messenger service called Beck and Call. He believes that there is no point in discussing the case, since the defendant's guilt is plain, and he is quick to insult and browbeat anyone who suggests otherwise. At one point, Juror Three describes how he fell out with his son. He raised his son to be tough, but when the boy was fifteen, he hit his father in the face, and Juror Three has not seen his son for three years. He condemns his son as ungrateful.

As the play develops, it becomes clear that Juror Three is the principal antagonist of Juror Eight. This is brought out visually when Juror Three demonstrates on Juror Eight how he would use a knife to stab a taller man. His animosity to Juror Eight comes out in the aggressive way he makes the demonstration, which shocks some of the jurors. Also, when Juror Eight calls him a sadist, Juror Three is incensed and threatens to kill him.

Juror Three is the last to hold out for a guilty verdict. For a few moments after it becomes apparent that he stands alone, he sticks to his guns, saying there will be a hung jury, but he finally gives in to the pressure and votes not guilty. In the film, he pulls out his wallet to produce some facts of the case—perhaps notes he has made—and a photograph of himself with his son falls out. He stares at it for a few moments and then tears it up and begins to sob. He recognizes that his desire to convict and punish the defendant is bound up with his feelings of anger and betrayal in regard to his own son.

Juror Four

Juror Four is described in the author's notes as seeming to be "a man of wealth and position, and a practiced speaker who presents himself well at all times." In the 1957 film, he is a stockbroker, a well-dressed man in an expensive suit who, unlike the others, does not remove his jacket and shows no signs of distress in the heat. He is an arch rationalist who insists that the jury should avoid emotional arguments in deciding the case. He has a good grasp of the facts and an excellent memory, and he presents the case for guilt as well as it can be done. He is extremely skeptical of the defendant's story that he was at the movies on the night of the murder. However, his pride in his memory is shaken when, under questioning from Juror Eight, he discovers that he cannot accurately recall the title of one of the movies he saw only a few days ago, nor can he remember the names of the actors. (This incident is not in the play, but it appears in the film.) However, he still believes strongly in the defendant's guilt and is the last juror but one to change his vote. This occurs when it is demonstrated that the piece of evidence on which he places greatest value—the woman's eyewitness testimony that she saw the murder take place—is undermined. He then admits that he has a reasonable doubt.

Juror Five

Juror Five is described in the author's notes as "a naive, very frightened young man who takes his obligations in this case very seriously but who finds it difficult to speak up when his elders have the floor." When, at the beginning, jurors are asked to speak in turn, Juror Five declines the opportunity. Later, he protests when Jurors Four and Ten speak disparagingly of kids from slum backgrounds, saying that he has lived in a slum all his life. Juror Five's main contribution is in pointing out that an experienced knife fighter would use a switchblade underhand, stabbing upward rather than down. He knows this because he has witnessed such fights. Juror Five is the second juror to switch his vote to not guilty. He acquires a reasonable doubt when it is shown that, because of the noise from the train, the old man could not have heard the boy yell that he would kill his father.

Juror Six

Juror Six is a housepainter, a man who is used to working with his hands rather than analyzing with his brain. He is more of a listener than a talker. In the film version, he suggests early in the debate that the defendant had a motive to kill his father, because there was testimony in the trial about an argument between father and son earlier in the evening. But Juror Eight dismisses this as a possible motive. Juror Six stands up for Juror Nine when Juror Three speaks rudely to him, threatening to strike Juror Three if he says anything like that again. Juror Six also speaks up for himself when he changes his vote, succinctly explaining why he did so. In the film version, he talks to Juror Eight in the washroom, asking him how he would feel if he succeeded in getting the defendant acquitted but later found out that he was guilty.

Juror Seven

Juror Seven is a salesman. He assumes that the defendant is guilty and has no interest in discussing it. His only concern is that the deliberations should be over quickly, so that he does not miss the Broadway show he has tickets for. (In the film version, he has tickets for a baseball game.) At no time does he make any serious contribution to the debate, other than to point out that the defendant has a record of arrests. In the film, he is a baseball fan and uses baseball allusions in almost everything he says. At one point, he gets into an argument with Juror Eleven about why Juror Eleven changed his vote, and he makes some prejudiced remarks about immigrants. He favors declaring a hung jury, because that will mean he will get out of the jury room quickly. Eventually, he changes his vote to not guilty, for the same reason. In the film version,

Juror Eleven harshly rebukes him for caring only about ending the proceedings as quickly as possible, rather than whether the man is guilty or not.

Juror Eight

Juror Eight is a quiet, thoughtful man whose main concern is that justice should be done. In the film, he is an architect. Although he is usually gentle in his manner, he is also prepared to be assertive in the search for truth. He is the only juror who, in the initial ballot, votes not guilty. He does not argue that the man is innocent but says that he cannot condemn a man to death without discussing the case first. As he probes the evidence, he manages to cast reasonable doubt on many aspects of the testimony given at the trial. He is resolute in suggesting that although, on its face, the evidence may suggest guilt, it is possible that there are other explanations for what happened that night. Juror Eight is a natural leader, and one by one he persuades the other jurors to accept his arguments. A telling moment comes when he produces a knife from his pocket that is exactly the same as the murder weapon; when he says that he bought it cheaply in the neighborhood, he disproves the jury's belief up to that point that the knife is a very unusual one.

Juror Eight remains calm throughout the deliberations. The only times (in the film version) that he becomes heated is when he stops the game of tic-tac-toe that Jurors Ten and Twelve have started and when he calls Juror Three a sadist. The latter incident serves his purpose, however, because it goads Juror Three into saying that he will kill Juror Eight, thus proving Juror Eight's earlier point that when such expression are used, they are not always meant literally.

Juror Nine

Juror Nine is an old man. In the author's notes, he is described as "long since defeated by life, and now merely waiting to die." In the film version, however, he is given more strength and dignity, and other jurors insist that he be heard. It is Juror Nine (in both play and film) who is the first to switch his vote to not guilty, saying that he wants a fuller discussion of the case, as Juror Eight has requested. It is Juror Nine who offers an explanation of why the old man might have lied about hearing the boy yell that he was going to kill his father. Juror Nine's explanation is that, because the old man has led an insignificant life and no one has ever taken any notice of him, this is his one chance for recognition. Juror Nine is also extremely observant, and the film version amplifies his role in the final discussion, when he is the one to point out that the female witness at the trial, in an effort to look younger, omitted to wear the glasses that she habitually wore, as shown by the marks on either side of her nose. This is the key point that results in the discrediting of the woman's testimony.

Juror Ten

Juror Ten is described in the author's notes as "an angry, bitter man—a man who antagonizes almost at sight. He is also a bigot." He is automatically prejudiced against anyone who comes from a slum. He believes strongly that the defendant is guilty, argues the case forcefully, and is one of the last three to hold out for a guilty verdict. But he loses credibility with the other jurors when he makes a long speech near the end of the play that reveals his bigotry in full. He insists that people from slums are drunks and liars who fight all the time. The other jurors repudiate him, and Juror Four tells him not to say another word; he does not, other than to finally admit that there is a reasonable doubt in the case.

Juror Eleven

Juror Eleven is an immigrant from Europe, a refugee from persecution. He is possibly Jewish, although this is not stated explicitly. In the film, he is a watchmaker. Juror Eleven feels fortunate to be living in a country known for its democracy, and he has great respect for the American judicial system. He takes his responsibility as a juror very seriously. He is one of three jurors who change their minds, to make the vote split six to six. He further expresses reasonable doubt about the old man's ability to recognize the son in a dimly lit tenement building. In the author's notes, he is described as "ashamed, humble, almost subservient to the people around him," but in the film his character is strengthened. He rebukes Juror Seven for not taking the trial more seriously, and he is prepared to stand up for what he believes. Also in the film version, he questions whether the son would have returned to his father's house at three o'clock in the morning if he had been the murderer.

Juror Twelve

Juror Twelve works for an advertising agency. He is clever, but as the author's notes point out, he "thinks of human beings in terms of percentages, graphs and polls, and has no real understanding of people." When Juror Three presses him, near the end of the play, to explain his not-guilty vote, he finds it very hard to do so, since he does not, in fact, have strong opinions one way or the other. He is reduced to mumbling about the complexity of the evidence.

The Triumph and the Fragility of Justice

The play is, in one sense, a celebration of justice, showing the workings of the American judicial system in a favorable light. Although initially the jury is inclined to wrongly convict a man without any discussion of the case, the persistence of Juror Eight ensures that the right verdict is reached in the end.

Three key elements of the judicial system are demonstrated in the play. The first is one that almost everyone knows, although Juror Eight has to remind Juror Two of it: According to the law, the defendant does not have to demonstrate his innocence. He is innocent until proved guilty. The second element is that the verdict must be unanimous, since unanimity guards against a miscarriage of justice. Third, the defendant can be convicted only in the absence of reasonable doubt on the part of the jury. If there is reasonable doubt, he must be acquitted. The underlying principle is that it is better that a guilty man be set free than an innocent man be convicted. In the film versions and at least one revival of the play, Juror Six, speaking to Juror Eight in the washroom, shows that he does not understand this principle, since he asks Juror Eight how he would feel if he managed to get the defendant acquitted and later found out that he was guilty (which he may be, since nothing that happens in the jury room proves his innocence). The system is as much about protecting the innocent as it is about convicting the guilty.

The play is also a warning about the fragility of justice and the forces of complacency, prejudice, and lack of civic responsibility that would undermine it. Several jurors show that they are virtually incapable of considering the matter fairly and listening to opposing points of view. Juror Seven, whose only desire is to get out of the room quickly, is clearly unfit for jury service. Juror Three insists that there is nothing personal in his negative comments about the defendant and that he is merely sticking to the facts. He denounces the arguments put forward by Juror Eight as emotional appeals. But there is an irony here, since the truth of Juror Three's position is the opposite of what he claims. He is dominated by his own emotions arising from his bad relationship with his son. Because of this, he cannot look at the case dispassionately. He harbors an unconscious desire to vicariously punish his son by convicting the defendant, who is of similar age. Juror Eight, on the other hand, refuses to let emotions interfere in the case. Unlike Juror Three and Juror Ten, the bigot, he brings no personal agenda to the deliberations and is solely interested in ensuring there is no miscarriage of justice. Whether the play is regarded as a celebration of justice or a warning about how easily justice can be subverted depends on one's views about the likelihood of a juror similar to Juror Eight being present in every jury room.

Overcoming Class and Race Prejudice

In the play, Juror Ten is violently prejudiced against anyone who comes from a slum. "You can't believe a word they say," he says early in act 1. Note that he does not say "he," meaning the defendant, but "they," the group as a whole, which shows that he cannot make a fair judgment about individual guilt. Juror Nine, the old man with much experience of life, sees this immediately and rebukes Juror Ten ("Since when is dishonesty a group characteristic?"). But Juror Ten's bigotry continues to smolder before finally erupting in a long speech near the end that leads the other jurors to reject him. The message is clear that such irrational prejudice is incompatible with justice. Juror Four also shows signs of such prejudice, though he couches it in more acceptable words: "The children who come out of slum backgrounds are potential menaces to society."

In the play, the defendant comes from a slum, but there is nothing to suggest that he is not white, as all the jurors are. In the 1957 film version, however, the defendant is shown in a fairly lengthy shot at the beginning. He is clearly Hispanic, perhaps Puerto Rican, and looks sad and vulnerable, rather different from the thug the jury initially believes him to be. The defendant as a member of an ethnic minority gives an entirely new, racial dimension to the notion of prejudice. The positive message is that in the end, prejudice is overcome in the light of reason, and perhaps those who express such prejudice are left to ponder how foolish and bigoted they have made themselves look. However, there is another, less positive way of seeing this issue. The ideal of the judicial system is that a person is judged by a jury of his peers, but the cross-section of white males on the jury can hardly be considered peers of the boy whose fate they are called upon to decide. It might also be argued that in showing the jurors almost to a man rejecting the blatant racial prejudice of Juror Ten (in a scene that is visually powerful onstage and onscreen), the playwright presents a rosy view of American society in the 1950s, which could hardly be said to be free of such prejudice against minorities or even to be willing to face up to the existence of it. Another view would argue that the playwright is aware of such social problems and is trying to educate his audience, encouraging them to see and reject attitudes that he has reason to believe many of them may hold.

Topics for Further Study

- Most states in the United States insist on a unanimous jury in criminal cases, but two states accept majority verdicts. Write an essay discussing the advantages and disadvantages of each method.

- Is a jury of ordinary people the best way to reach a correct verdict in a trial? Would a panel of judges or other legal experts be a better way? Research a trial in which the jury reached a controversial verdict and write a letter to the editor of your local newspaper discussing these issues.

- In what ways do Jurors Eight, Nine, and Eleven embody the ideal of active citizenship in a democracy?

What kinds of threats to the success of democracy through active citizen participation are posed by Jurors Three, Seven, Ten, and Twelve? Team up with two other classmates and make a class presentation in which you discuss these issues.

- In the play and the 1957 film, the jury is all-white and all-male. In the 1997 remake of the film, four jurors are African American. There are no women in any versions of the play. Should race and gender play a part in jury selection? Would female jurors or Hispanic jurors have been less willing to convict the defendant in *Twelve Angry Men*? Set up a classroom debate in which one person argues in favor of taking race and gender into account and the other person argues against it.

- Watch the 1957 and the 1997 film versions of *Twelve Angry Men*. Give a class presentation, with clips from the movies if possible, outlining the major differences between the two versions. Do you prefer Henry Fonda's performance as Juror Eight, or Jack Lemmon's? Compare and contrast the ways at least two other jurors are presented.

Democracy and Social Responsibility

The play suggests that not only must class and race prejudice be overcome, so must political differences. Juror Eight adopts a classic liberal position. He tries to understand the social background from which the defendant came, explaining the boy's anger as a reaction to his social conditions: "You know why slum kids get that way? Because we knock 'em over the head once a day, every day." Jurors Three, Four, and Ten adopt a more conservative position. They have no sympathy with examining the social causes of crime and simply want to get tough on the criminal. But the play shows that both liberal and conservative positions are essentially irrelevant in deciding whether the boy is guilty. The jurors must transcend their political differences and work together to find out the truth. In this sense, the play is a microcosm of democracy at work. Everyone has their say, and everyone works together to further the common good, which, in this case, is the administration of justice. It is Juror Eleven who makes this connection between the American judicial system and the democracy that, as an immigrant, he loves and respects because it is so different from what he knew in his home country. He emphasizes that everyone must play their part in it: "We have a responsibility. This is a remarkable thing about democracy…. We have nothing to gain or lose by our verdict. This is one of the reasons why we are strong."

Style

Limited Setting, Claustrophobic Atmosphere

The play has only one setting, the jury room, though both films and later stage productions added a washroom. Props are minimal, consisting mainly of a long conference table and twelve chairs. The room is hot and humid, since there is no air-conditioning and the fan does not work. The atmosphere is claustrophobic, and the men are understandably short-tempered. This confined setting helps produce the basic rhythm of the play: a juror or several jurors will provide exposition, reviewing some of the details of the case, and this will be followed by a flare-up, in which jurors express sharp disagreements and engage in bad-tempered exchanges. These, in turn, are followed by a quieter phase as tempers calm, before more exposition sets the rhythm in motion again. In this way, the static setting, in which no one comes or goes, is overcome by the dramatic rhythm inherent in the dialogue. The static setting is also mitigated by the way the director has the actors move around the stage as the arguments ebb and flow.

In the 1957 film version, the heat of the room is conveyed by the jurors shown with their shirts visibly stained with sweat. This also contributes to characterization, since Juror Four, who remains calm and rational throughout, does not sweat. After the thunderstorm cools the room a little, the sweat dries up, except in the case of Juror Three, which conveys something about his tense, emotional state of mind.

Film provides opportunities a stage director does not have; in the film, the director Sidney Lumet achieves movement and variety by frequently varying the camera angles. The changes in camera angles multiply as the dramatic tension increases. Also, Lumet progressively lowers the level from which the movie is shot. The first third is shot from above eye level, the second third at eye level, and the last third from below eye level. In the last third, the ceiling of the room begins to appear, giving a sense that the room is getting smaller.

Lumet's use of progressively longer lenses also contributes to the seeming diminishment of the room. Lumet began with normal-range lenses of 28 to 40 millimeters and then progressed to 50-, 75-, and 100-millimeter lenses. (The length of the lens refers to the focal length, or the distance from the focal point to the lens.) The longer lens alters the relationships of subject and background, giving the impression in the film that the walls are closing in and also making the table look more crowded, thus adding to the atmosphere of claustrophobia.

Live Television Drama in the 1950s

The decade of the 1950s is sometimes known as the golden era of television, largely because thousands of live dramas were broadcast during that time. These dramas supplemented the standard television fare of variety shows, westerns, and soap operas. It was during this period that television replaced radio and film as the chief medium of entertainment for the American family.

The live programs were in the form of drama anthologies, such as NBC's *Kraft Television Theater* and *Goodyear Television Playhouse* and CBS's *Studio One*. It was *Studio One*, which ran from 1948 to 1958, that aired *Twelve Angry Men* and other plays by Rose. Rose recalled in an interview the challenging but rewarding nature of television drama in the 1950s: "It was a terrifying experience, but very exhilarating. But there were always mistakes…. I don't recall a show I ever did when something didn't go wrong" (quoted in "Reginald Rose: A Biography," in *Readings on "Twelve Angry Men,"* edited by Russ Munyan). Rose recalls cameras breaking down and shows that ran either too long or too short to fill the exact time slot allocated.

There was great variety in the content of these dramas. Some were adaptations of stage plays by such playwrights as Eugene O'Neill and Arthur Miller as well as Shakespeare. Most, however, were original dramas. The constant demand for new plays provided a fruitful creative outlet for writers, directors, and actors in the new medium. Television drama offered actors who were not well known in movies their first national exposure. In 1949, Marlon Brando, then only twenty-four years old, starred in *I'm No Hero*, a television drama produced by the Actors Studio. Paul Newman and Steve McQueen made appearances on the *Goodyear Television Playhouse*. Directors such as John Frankenheimer, Robert Altman, Sidney Lumet, and Sidney Pollack, who would later become known for their work in film, began their careers directing television dramas in the late 1940s and 1950s. Live drama died out in the early 1960s, because new technology enabled productions to be filmed. This produced higher-quality technical work, since mistakes could be edited out and scenes could be reshot, but many of the pioneer actors, writers, and directors bemoaned the loss of the excitement and intimacy of live drama.

Compare & Contrast

- **1950s:** In 1953, 55 percent of American households possess a television set. In 1955, the figure jumps to 67 percent. In this year, 7,421,084 television sets are sold in the United States. NBC is the first network to have a regularly scheduled color program on the air (*Bonanza*, starting in 1959).

Today: More than 98 percent of households have television sets, and many have more than one. In 1999, 68 percent of households with television have cable television. On average, Americans watch four hours of television a day.

- **1950s:** Support for the death penalty in the United States drops. In the 1940s, there were, on average, nearly 130 executions a year, but in the 1950s this figure falls to an average of 71.5 executions. The most famous cases are those of Julius and Ethel Rosenberg, who are put to death in New York in 1953 for passing atomic secrets to the Soviet Union. In New York in 1954, the year *Twelve Angry Men* is first televised, nine people are executed. Two of the condemned are teenagers; a total of three more teenagers die in New York's Sing Sing in 1955 and 1956.

Today: Although the United States is one of the few countries to retain the death penalty, the number of executions is falling, from 71 in 2002 to 65 in 2003 and 59 in 2004.

In New York, Governor George Pataki reinstates the death penalty in 1995, but, as of 2005, New York had not executed anyone since 1963. In 2005, the Supreme Court abolished the death penalty for those who commit murder when younger than age eighteen. This decision affects not only future sentencing but also approximately seventy prisoners on death row who were under eighteen when they committed their crimes.

- **1950s:** The cold war between the United States and the Soviet Union dominates global politics in the era, as does the Korean War, from 1950 to 1953. Fear of Communism leads to the McCarthy era in the United States. Television drama during this period often includes patriotic sentiments, such as those expressed by Juror Eleven in *Twelve Angry Men*. There is a perceived need to reinforce U.S. citizens' belief in the virtues of American democracy in contrast to the totalitarian Communist states of China and the Soviet Union.

Today: The cold war is over, leaving the United States as the sole superpower. U.S. and, to an extent, global politics are dominated by the "war on terror." The Islamic terrorist group al Qaeda has replaced the Soviet Union in the minds of Americans as the prime source of evil in the world. Politicians regularly exploit people's fear of terrorism to gain support for their policies.

McCarthyism and Fear of Communism

In the 1950s, during the cold war between the United States and the Soviet Union, Americans were apprehensive about the spread of Communism around the world and at home. The Communist takeover of China in 1949, as well as the U.S.S.R.'s first test explosion of an atomic bomb that same year, followed by the Communist invasion of Korea in 1950, had all intensified these fears. In the late 1940s, the House Un-American Activities Committee (HUAC) began to investigate people who were suspected of being Communists. Their focus was on Hollywood and the entertainment industry. In October 1947, nineteen witnesses called before HUAC refused to cooperate with the committee; as a result, ten of them, who became known as the Hollywood Ten, were sentenced in 1950 to between six and twelve months in prison. During the 1950s, many people who worked in film, theater, radio, and television were blacklisted for alleged ties to Communism. They were prevented from working again in the entertainment industry.

The 1950s also saw the rise of Joseph McCarthy, a Republican senator from Wisconsin and a fierce anti-Communist. In 1950, McCarthy claimed that he had a list of 205 Communists who worked in the U.S. State Department. The following year, McCarthy became chairman of the Senate Subcommittee on Investigations, which gave him even greater authority to pursue suspected Communists. Many people lost their jobs as a result of admitting that they were members of the Communist Party. Some, in order to show they had renounced their left-wing views, gave information about others who were Communist Party members.

Having created an atmosphere of hysteria regarding Communist infiltration and conspiracies, McCarthy overreached himself when he began to investigate Communist infiltration of the U.S. military, which angered military leaders as well as President Dwight Eisenhower, a retired general. From April to June 1954, the Army-McCarthy hearings were televised and watched by an estimated twenty million viewers. When *Twelve Angry Men* was shown only three months later, on September 20, 1954, viewers could hardly fail to see the contrast in the play's theme of fairness and justice with the witch hunt led by McCarthy. In December 1954, McCarthy was censured by the U.S. Senate, and the McCarthy era essentially came to an end.

Critical Overview

When *Twelve Angry Men* was first shown as a live television drama on CBS in 1954, Leonard Traube, in *Variety*, wrote one of the first of the many positive reviews the play was to receive. As he puts it, "Seldom in TV history has a story been able to achieve so many high points with such frequency and maintain the absorbing, tense pace."

When Rose revised the play and coproduced a movie version with Henry Fonda in 1957, critical response was also positive. The reviewer for *Newsweek* calls the film a "hard, emphatic, single-minded drama of extraordinary drive and fascination." In *America*, Moira Walsh describes it as "continuously absorbing…. It is well constructed and abounds in forceful and abrasive characterizations." However, the film was not an immediate popular success and was quickly withdrawn from large theaters. Subsequently, it was shown at the Berlin Film Festival, where it won first prize. It also won prizes in Japan, Italy, Australia, and other countries. Since then, it has established a reputation as one of the significant films of the 1950s and an all-time American classic film.

Revised by Rose, the play was revived in 1996 at the Comedy Theatre in London, directed by the noted British playwright and director Harold Pinter. The reviewer Matt Wolf, in *Variety*, finds the play a "startlingly innocent work in its belief in a fundamental integrity to the legal process." He contrasts this with the disillusionment felt by many in the United States in the mid-1990s, after the controversial acquittal of O. J. Simpson on double-murder charges in 1995.

The play was revived again at the American Airlines Theater in New York in 2004. John Simon, writing in *New York*, praises the strong writing and the characterization and the "underlying faith in democratic procedure not neutralizing the frightful precariousness of its realization." He concludes:

> This superficially dated but fundamentally self-renewing play is more than a lesson in civics and shrewd analysis of a cross-section of psyches. It is a nudge toward our leaving the theater a bit better than we entered it.

Sources

American Civil Liberties Union (ACLU), "Inadequate Representation," http://www.aclu.org/DeathPenalty/DeathPenalty.cfm ID=9313&c=62 (posted October 8, 2003).

Cutler, Brian L., and Stephen D. Penrod, *Mistaken Identification: The Eyewitness, Psychology, and the Law*, Cambridge University Press, 1995, p. 12.

Ellsworth, Phoebe C., Review of *Twelve Angry Men*, in *Michigan Law Review*, Vol. 101, No. 6, May 2003, pp. 1387-1407.

"Inside the Jury Room," in *Newsweek*, April 15, 1957, p. 113.

Loftus, Elizabeth F., *Eyewitness Testimony*, Harvard University Press, 1979, pp. 1-7, 9-10, 171-74.

"Reginald Rose: A Biography," in *Readings on "Twelve Angry Men,"* edited by Ross Munyan, Greenhaven Press, 2000, p. 19.

Rose, Reginald, "Author's Commentary," in *Six Television Plays*, Simon and Schuster, 1956, p. 156.

——————————, *Twelve Angry Men: A Play in Three Acts*, Dramatic Publishing Company, 1955, pp. 4-5, 15, 16, 21, 22, 44, 45, 60.

Simon, John, "No Doubt," in *New York*, Vol. 37, No. 39, pp. 71-72.

Smith, David Burnell, "*Twelve Angry Men* Presents an Idealized View of the Jury System," in *Readings on "Twelve Angry Men,"* edited by Ross Munyan, Greenhaven Press, 2000, pp. 97-101.

Traube, Leonard, "The 1954 Production Was Excellent Television Drama," in *Readings on "Twelve Angry Men,"* edited by Ross Munyan, Greenhaven Press, 2000, p. 108; originally published in *Variety*, September 24, 1954.

Walsh, Moira, Review of *Twelve Angry Men*, in *America*, April 27, 1957, p. 150.

Wolf, Matt, "The 1996 London Stage Version Is Timely," in *Readings on "Twelve Angry Men,"* edited by Ross Munyan, Greenhaven Press, 2000, p. 122; originally published in *Variety*, May 20-26, 1996.

Further Reading

Abramson, Jeffrey, *We the Jury: The Jury System and the Ideal of Democracy*, with a new preface, Harvard University Press, 2000.

> Abramson, who is a former prosecutor, describes the history and function of juries in democratic society. He discusses such issues as mandatory cross-section representation for juries and scientific jury selection and advocates mandatory unanimous verdicts. He concludes that the jury system works well and serves the interests of democracy.

Burnett, D. Graham, *A Trial by Jury*, Vintage, 2002.

> Burnett, a historian of science, was the foreman of the jury in a murder trial in New York City, and in this book he discusses the responsibilities and frustrations of jury duty. The result is an excellent account of what really goes on in a jury room. Reviewers made comparisons between this book and *Twelve Angry Men*.

Hans, Valerie P., and Neil Vidmar, *Judging the Jury*, Perseus, 2001.

The authors discuss the performance of juries and conclude that on the whole, they do a competent job. Other issues discussed in the book include jury selection, the effects of prejudice, and the significance of whether the verdict is unanimous or a majority decision. They also cover the history and development of the jury system.

Yarmey, A. Daniel, *The Psychology of Eyewitness Testimony*, Free Press, 1979.

Yarmey presents the psychological and legal aspects of eyewitness identification. He also discusses the implications for criminal justice of the scientific literature on memory, perception, and social perception.